COUNTRY · EXPLORERS ·

GW00993664

A Visit to

AUSTRALIA

by Charis Mather

BEARPORT
PUBLISHING

Minneapolis, Minnesota

Credits

All images are courtesy of Shutterstock.com, unless otherwise specified. With thanks to Getty Images, Thinkstock Photo, and iStockphoto.

Cover – ChameleonsEye, Travelling.About. 2–3 – Camille Forster. 4–5 – Olga Kashubin, Johan Swanepoel. 6–7 – Thomas Edmondson, Maz Day. 8–9 – Hans Wagemaker, Korawee Ratchapakdee. 10–11 – Benny Marty, Maurizio De Mattei, Aldo Manganaro. 12–13 – J Mundy, ChameleonsEye. 14–15 – pierdest, ChameleonsEye. 16–17 – Aaronejbull87, lavizzara, Imagine Earth Photography. 18–19 – Wonderly Imaging, rickyd, petrdd, Jason Benz Bennee. 20–21 – matteo_it, Batkova Elena. 22–23 – Alvov, Andrea Izzotti.

Library of Congress Cataloging-in-Publication Data is available at www.loc.gov or upon request from the publisher.

ISBN: 979-8-88509-036-0 (hardcover)
ISBN: 979-8-88509-047-6 (paperback)
ISBN: 979-8-88509-058-2 (ebook)

© 2023 Booklife Publishing
This edition is published by arrangement with Booklife Publishing.

For more information, write to Bearport Publishing, 5357 Penn Avenue South, Minneapolis, MN 55419. Printed in the United States of America.

CONTENTS

COUNTRY TO COUNTRY

Which country do you live in?

A country is an area of land marked by **borders**. The people in each country have their own rules and ways of living. They may speak different languages.

Each country around the world has its own interesting things to see and do. Let's take a trip to visit a country and learn more!

Have you ever visited another country?

5

TODAY'S TRIP IS TO
AUSTRALIA!

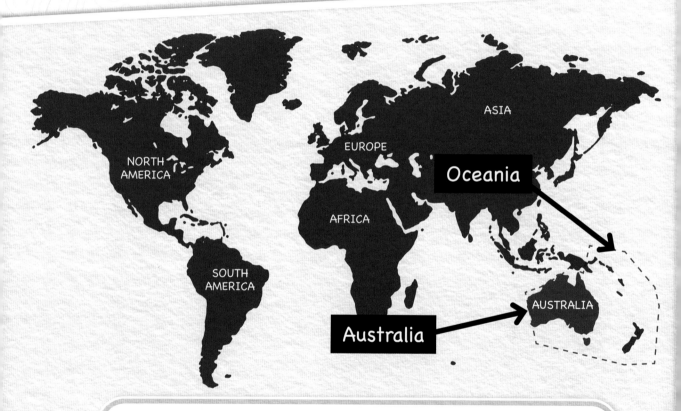

Australia is a country that is also a **continent**. It is part of a region called Oceania. This area includes Australia and nearby islands.

FACT FILE

Capital city: Canberra
Main language: English
Currency:
Australian dollar
Flag:

Currency is the type of money that is used in a country.

SYDNEY

We'll start our trip in the city of Sydney, near the Sydney Harbor Bridge. Trains and cars pass over this 1,650-foot (500-m) long bridge. People walk across it, too.

This bridge is sometimes called the coat hanger because of its shape.

Sydney also has the famous Sydney Opera House. Millions of people from across the world visit this beautiful building. They watch performers play music, sing, give speeches, and put on plays.

ULURU

Next, let's go see Uluru! It is a large rock made of **sandstone**. Uluru is known for its impressive size and color. Sometimes, it looks bright red, especially in the evening.

In the evening

In the daytime

Uluru is about 1,150 ft (350 m) tall.

While many people visit Uluru, this place has special meaning to some **Aboriginal** Australians. Uluru is important in some of their stories.

Aboriginal rock art can be found on Uluru.

ABORIGINAL TRADITIONS

The Yolngu people celebrate by dancing.

Australia has many groups of Aboriginal people, each with their own traditions. These ways of living have been passed down in the groups for many years. It is important to always remember these traditions.

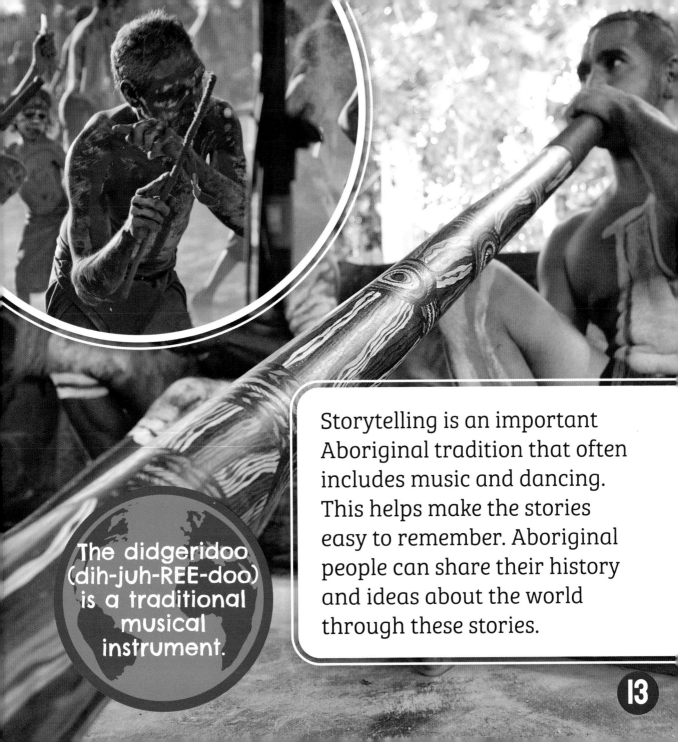

The didgeridoo (dih-juh-REE-doo) is a traditional musical instrument.

Storytelling is an important Aboriginal tradition that often includes music and dancing. This helps make the stories easy to remember. Aboriginal people can share their history and ideas about the world through these stories.

13

ABORIGINAL ART

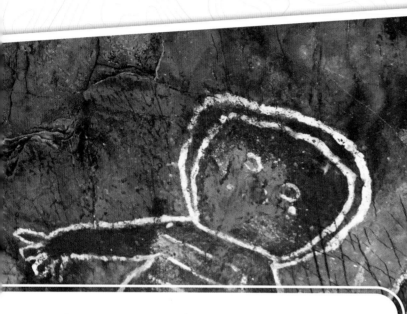

Aboriginal people also share traditional stories through art. Different groups have different ways to make art. Some use dots or lines to make patterns. They may paint on rocks or bark.

As a sign of respect, other artists do not copy Aboriginal art.

Symbols such as arrows, rings, and wavy lines are used to add meaning to art. Rings inside rings might mean a place to stay or a place with water. An upside-down U might stand for a person.

GREAT BARRIER REEF

Next, let's go to the Great Barrier Reef. This underwater wonder is made of **coral**. It is home to fish, dolphins, sea turtles, and many other living things.

The Great Barrier Reef can be seen from space.

Sea turtle

Humpback whale

The Great Barrier Reef gets some large visitors. Humpback whales travel there to **mate**. The whales then have their babies at the reef.

17

ANIMALS

Kangaroo

Koala

Tasmanian devil

Australia also has amazing animals on land. Let's meet the kangaroo, the koala, and the Tasmanian devil. These animals all come from Australia.

Tasmanian devils sometimes bite each other. *Ouch!*

The Tasmanian devil is small, but it has a big head. This gives it a strong bite for its size. The Tasmanian devil often eats animals that are already dead.

LAKE HILLIER

Lake Hillier is always pink.

Now, let's hop in an airplane to see Lake Hillier. This pink lake is on an island in Western Australia. Visitors are not normally allowed to walk near the lake, so they fly planes over it instead. Lake Hillier's pink color is best seen from above.

No one knows for sure why the lake is so pink. Some people think it is because of the amount of salt in the water. Lake Hillier is even saltier than the nearby ocean.

Lake Hillier is so salty that no fish or plants can live in it.

BEFORE YOU GO

Great Ocean Road

We can't forget to drive on the Great Ocean Road! This route along the ocean has some fantastic sights, including rocky cliffs and beautiful forests.

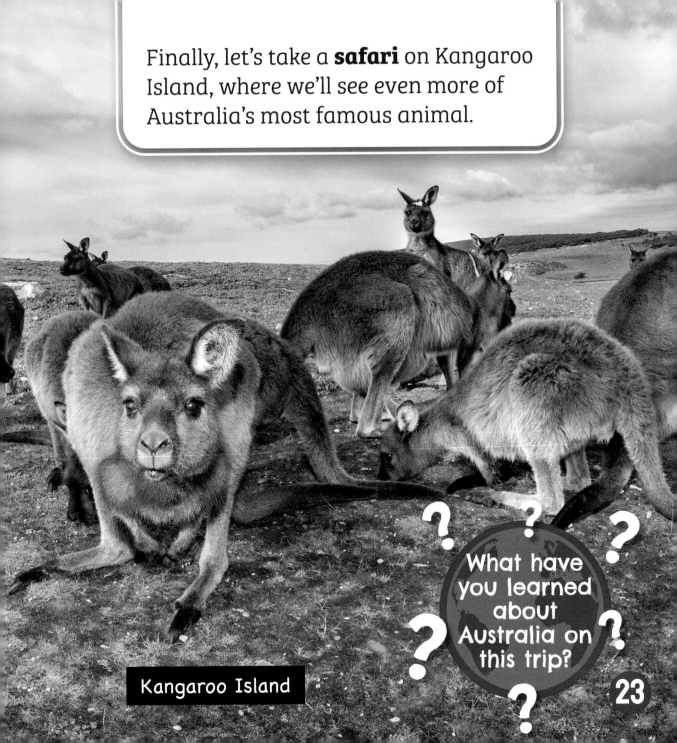

Finally, let's take a **safari** on Kangaroo Island, where we'll see even more of Australia's most famous animal.

Kangaroo Island

What have you learned about Australia on this trip?

23

GLOSSARY

Aboriginal having to do with the first people to ever live in Australia

borders lines that show where one place ends and another begins

continent one of the world's seven large land masses

coral rocklike structures on the bottom of the ocean made from skeletons of small animals

mate to come together to have young

safari a trip to see animals in their natural habitat

sandstone a type of rock

INDEX